FROM
SHIFTING
SAND
TO
SOLID
ROCK

FROM SHIFTING SAND TO SOLID ROCK

MELVIN JOHN RUOHONEN

From Shifting Sand to Solid Rock
Copyright © 2021 by Melvin John Ruohonen. All rights reserved.

No part of this publication may be reproduced, stored in a retrieval system or transmitted in any way by any means, electronic, mechanical, photocopy, recording or otherwise without the prior permission of the author except as provided by USA copyright law.

The opinions expressed by the author are not necessarily those of URLink Print and Media.

1603 Capitol Ave., Suite 310 Cheyenne, Wyoming USA 82001
1-888-980-6523 | admin@urlinkpublishing.com

URLink Print and Media is committed to excellence in the publishing industry.

Book design copyright © 2021 by URLink Print and Media. All rights reserved.

Published in the United States of America

Library of Congress Control Number: 2021912436
ISBN 978-1-64753-849-1 (Paperback)
ISBN 978-1-64753-850-7 (Digital)

02.06.21

SPECIAL ACKNOWLEDGEMENT

It is with overwhelming conviction that I recognize key, talented people who were involved in the preparation of my book, which I consider to be "teaching memoirs." Even more I would encourage all members of our current government administration to learn from this process. It is the work of true entrepreneurs reaching for our leader, Tate Publishing, to complete our American Dream. Our developmental format was as The Constitution of the United States portrays.

I hand wrote this book over eight years. Karen Hostetter of Melbourne, Florida, transferred my notes to computer, and Jean A. Milakovich from Ironwood, Michigan, pre-edited the book. Kalyn McAlister final edited the works for production. These people are extremely talented. It is the way our country should operate. I asked "Jeannie" to offer her input in the production of my book.

"Thank you to Mary Elaine Harris for being the photo master, enabling the reading public to see a glimpse of the Butterfly".

"Special consideration to Sherry Ross of URlink Print and Media for the deep understanding of the author and putting his thoughts into words."

—Melvin John Ruohonen

THE AUTHOR. THE BUTTERFLY. THE BOOK.

I have known "Mel" Ruohonen for over thirty years. We have always been friends. In 1991 I had a conversation with Mel about his desire to write a book. Mel was dedicated to use his life to teach others about loss, love, and life in general. I offered to edit the book.

Many people say they would like to do things in life, but never do. Mel is the exception. In 2008 he sent me the beginning chapters. His draft was roughly written and I immediately worked on finding his paper voice." Over one hundred hours were put in, using the computer and phone to communicate because he lives in Florida, and I, in Michigan.

Once my work was done, I told Mel of a poem that I wrote about the life cycle. Parts of my poem reminded me of Mel. We are so different. I choose the cautious, watchful approach to ventures. Mel "takes the plunge." When he reaches a precipice, he just leaps to the other side. I have always respected that; though I believe it has caused him much heartache.

All of us sink into darkness at times; some never resurface. It is with the eternal light in Mel's life the strength of his faith has always saved him when he crashed.

—Jean A. Milakovich

NOTE: Poem Written FOR AUTHOR from friend of 30 years. (Her perception Of The Author)

FLY ON

Every life is a butterfly
Flitting briefly across our field of sight;
We rejoice in its emergence,
Celebrate the beauty of its unique colors and patterns
As it lights softly on field or flower.

We learn too soon that we cannot hold it,
No matter how much we desire that;
We watch helplessly as it flies
away, But we remember
And hope it flies on.

To another field,
Another flower,
Beyond the limited range
Of human vision, Human understanding

Jeannie Milakovich

PREFACE

From shifting sand to solid rock is the perfect metaphor for my life. I attribute my life to two entities. One is my father, who wanted me to have opportunities he never had, and the second is my relationship with God.

The wind has blown me around, and little did I know that God and my family were with me. There may have been one set of footprints in the sand, but I was never alone. God has intervened in my life on four different occasions. When a long-distance runner gets his second wind, everything seems to light up and he feels more energy. The messages from God come in the same way to me. I have had and lost much in my life. God's interventions have saved me.

I don't desire much anymore. Now sixty-two, all I want is a complete relationship with my daughters and an opportunity to be part of my grandchildren's lives. My message for my daughters is that I sincerely apologize for any pain my actions have caused them, I miss them and pray daily that there is an understanding that allows full reconciliation of a relationship. The precipitator of both may have to be some tragedy or another heavenly intervention. As difficult as relationships can be, I hand it all to Him. I make my own decisions and am responsible for them. Thank you, God, for not judging me and for your great forgiveness.

My writing is influenced by two books that answered most of my metaphysical questions about life. The first is

The Shack by William P. Young. The shack is a symbol of my beliefs. Jesus is my best friend, and my relationship with God is exciting. I was amazed how I have envisioned my life as represented in Mr. Young's work. God encouraged me to sing, dance, and most of all, laugh. My entire life has been dedicated to helping people see the beauty in their person and their surroundings and to always appreciate God's gifts. How do you think God feels when we worship in so many different ways, with so many different churches? If Jesus were to return today, which church would He attend?

The second book, Freedom from Spirituality, is written by C. Peter Marshall. I believe this work represents correct discernment about people, churches, and pastors. Church has been difficult for me recently. Having attended services from conservative Lutheran to very liberal. Pentecostal, I struggle with so many people talking the talk, but not walking the walk. Currently I attend a non-denominational church, formerly Baptist. I no longer look for pastoral leadership, but a desire for biblical education.

Because so many experiences in my life were hindered by over zealous parishes, my focus goes on messages that are biblically driven. I have found that people who say they represent God usually have a personal agenda also. Only when I started to attend service and prayer groups did I learn to only listen to the many different interpretations and realize that the true art of worship is my discernment, not those of parishioners or clergy.

I believe that security in direction of life has to be in a relationship with Jesus. Lay people who are educated to be a messenger of God's word are people just like you and me. We are all sinners and are subject to personal views and interpretations of the Word. Now, when I hear the message,

I am excited to talk to my best friend in prayer to review in Scripture what was represented by our teachers in church. In the book of Samuel, I lean toward several small sections. I refer to Chapter 9, verse 3 and verse 20. My quote based on the readings in Samuel is, "Never chase your donkeys; always ask where your donkeys are." In definition, complete the work and hand it over to Jesus to bring to our Father. Always remember that your wishes may not be His way. My father used to say to be careful what you pray for, you might get it. God knows best.

When I reached this point in my life the wind stopped and the sand began to crystallize. There is a hymn called "On Solid Ground a Church Will Stand, Not One Built on Shifting Sand." As you follow my words in the writings, I challenge you to feel the transition, the settling, and the formation of the Rock.

FOOTINGS

Weather in Northern Michigan can come in the form of all four seasons in just one week. Oskar, Michigan, a small farming community north of Houghton and my birthplace, is no exception. I am a member of the Ruohonen and Carlson families, who produced twenty-one children. My father, Hjalmer Ruohonen, had thirteen siblings; my mother, Minetha Carlson Ruohonen, had six. My grandfather, who never spoke English, led a small group of people from Finland to the woods of northern Michigan. I have my own, somewhat troublesome moniker. My name is Melvin John Ruohonen. That name and my Yooper (Upper Peninsula of Michigan) heritage began on June 23, 1947.

Of course, I affected Mom and Dad's life too. My birth was difficult for Mom, and she literally spent two years pacing due to my susceptibility to tonsillitis and croup. Dad worried about adequately providing for his family and worked several jobs in Houghton County, everything from furnace repair to construction. I once asked Dad why I was the only child. Dad never really said. The Finnish people fiercely protect their privacy. Sometimes, their efforts to do so are thwarted though. My paternal grandparents never spoke English, but I learned enough Finnish to translate some conversations—especially when the topic was Christmas presents.

Most of my family still lives in rural Oskar, a very small town west of Portage Lake and about six miles north of Houghton, Michigan. The town was named for Oskar Eliasson, a Finnish lumberman who once owned and operated a sawmill there. In addition to lumbering, the Finnish operated farms, though at one time, little Oskar even had a tannery. Today, my cousins work at the university or the surrounding small businesses.

Because my mother was allergic to animals, my nuclear family moved to Elevation Street in Hancock, Michigan. One block away lived my cousin and best friend, Janine Sanartto. She and I often walked to Lompre's Market with a nickel to spend.

Janine always bought Juicy Fruit. I favored bubble gum because of the sports cards. Janine and I played dolls together too. I had a boy doll, of course. I've always joked that I was 60 percent female because I rely so heavily on intuition. Unfortunately, those insights would take time to develop.

At the end of the summer of 1953, Janine and I prepared to enter E. L. Wright Elementary School in Hancock, Michigan. We went to town in late summer to get school supplies, Parents always wanted to choose clothing. My Big Mac overalls from Gartner's Department Store solicited hoots of derision from my new classmates.

"Melvin looks funny!"

"Melvin is a farmer!"

"Look at Melvin's suspenders and the big pockets in his pants!"

Every time the teacher called out my name, "Mellllvinnn"—I wished I was back in Oskar.

Gail Johannson was the only bright spot that first year. Gail had blonde hair, glasses, and the most beautiful pigtails

I had ever seen. Our kindergarten teacher built a cardboard school bus for us to play in during free time. One day, Gail and I were in the bus alone when I garnered enough courage to kiss her on the cheek. My heart was beating so fast I could hardly breathe. I was in love. I couldn't wait until the next day. To my dismay, the next day was Saturday and I would have to wait two whole days to see Gail. My aggressive love relationship with Gail was short lived as my eyes began to wander in search of more challenges. One kiss on Gail's cheek started my Kindergarten reputation as available. I think my suspenders were the reason. Sexy, whatever that word means to a five-year-old.

On Saturday, around 5:00 p.m., our family of three would go to the Alatalos for sauna, a Finnish steam bath. Dad said a sauna opened up the pores and helped us sweat out all the dirt we had accumulated during the week. The temperature was so hot that I put a cold washcloth over my face to breathe. Cleaning out my pores became a weekly ritual. I never considered putting myself in an oven "good for me." What I did savor was the warm Finnish flatbread with butter and Nesbitt's orange soda that followed saunas. I always drank mine slowly. When the parents started to play Pinochle, Ricky and I went outside.

I would meet Ricky behind Alatalo's garage. Ricky lived on Quincy Hill, gateway to the beautiful Keweenaw Peninsula, a tourist haven. When travelers tossed their lit cigarettes out of the window, Ricky and I would pick them up to smoke. A good day was when someone tossed a cigar. It was exciting to do this. What followed was something I have dealt with all of my life. It was wrong. My conscience was killing me. The Lutheran Church and my parents influence created a very active conscience. Smoking a cigarette was a sin. I was going to hell. As the book introduces the marriages in my life the reader will see that the women are great people. My conscience created such a tunnel vision lead by guilt I had no idea what true love was.

Apostolic Lutherans had predictable Sundays. Church lasted for one hour—the longest hour in the week. Church behavior was required: be very quiet, recite together, sing songs that bordered on funeral marches, give money, and go home. The humorous part of life was as I get older, the funeral hymns are some of my favorites. Could it be that my parents were getting smarter? After church, we settled in for meat, potatoes, and peas. I didn't like peas. I was encouraged to eat my peas. Dad said to remember all of the people in India who didn't have peas. I silently thought they could have mine.

Work in Houghton County was difficult for dad to find. Once I finished kindergarten, we moved seventy miles west to White Pine, Michigan. Dad would work in an underground copper mine. The move was not very difficult. My parents did not fit in comfortably with family. Relatives were either far right in church beliefs or opening the local bars each day. On the Carlson side, most moved to Detroit for work.

The Carlson side, most notably my Uncle Hugo, is credited for my "live, love, and laugh" attitude in life. Hugo, Uncle Alphonse, and Uncle John taught me how to play poker and place bets at Hazel Park Raceway. The two families obviously didn't gather for holiday dinners.

My father was a "mugwump"-a political reference to his mug on one side and his wump on the other. It's my way of telling you that Dad was an independent; his beliefs weren't opposed to a moderate lifestyle (somewhere between the two extremes of the other relatives). I really appreciate that temperance. I never saw my parents use alcohol. Rumors exist that Dad used to "tip a few" before he married Mom. In fact, a tipsy Dad supposedly once acted like a traffic cop on Woodward Avenue in Detroit.

Until I was fifteen, I believed in God mostly because my parents put me in Sunday school and, through guilt, I went to church every Sunday, If I did anything wrong, my conscience took over. Fear and guilt controlled my life.

GROWING PAINS

My first day of kindergarten may have been the last day I took studying seriously. School was fun when recess, lunch, and playtime came around. Reading, spelling, and history were somewhat interesting. My fifth-grade teacher, Mrs. Jolkanen, was really interesting, one of my favorites unfortunately for the wrong reasons. Mrs. Jolkanen was a young woman with large breasts. The strap for her bra kept slipping down, and I wanted so much to help her with the problem. I spent the entire 180 plus days of the school year watching those breasts. This time, I told my conscience to go away.

What does a sissy look like? Before I left elementary school, I was the epitome. I continued to wear Big Mac pants and suspenders. Add to that Converse "red ball jets," the red basketball shoes, and a bowl haircut, and you get a complete picture of Melvin in those years. To make matters even worse, my body was beginning to develop—just one section at a time. I had the backside and legs of an athlete and the arms of an anorexic. When my gym teacher barked, "Melvin it's your turn to climb the rope," I just couldn't do it. First of all, I was afraid of heights. More importantly, I couldn't believe anyone actually expected my little engine to pull a big caboose especially up.

Of course the bullies noted my failures. Between classes, Charley Lantto and Mike Biodo shoved their elbows in my ribs every day after each class. They scared me, and I wasn't free of their taunts, even after regular hours. Every Monday night, after the elementary school movie, I had to run home because the Cherry Road gang, which included Mike and Charley, wanted to hurt me. I kept thinking, Someday, it will be my turn! My turn wouldn't happen for quite a while.

As you might guess, elementary school was not a pleasant time of my life. In fact, between the teachers' bellowing, "Melllviin," Chipmunks-fashion and the other students' taunts, I was miserable. Sure, I enjoyed sports, music, and social clubs; but peer pressure plagued me. I was always anxious about being cornered in combative, abusive situations. I was afraid of getting beat up or ridiculed in public. Every time I thought I had planted my feet on solid ground, the ground shifted, leaving me as insecure and afraid as I had been before.

ADOLESCENT ANGST AND PROMISE

Seventh grade offered some promise; and once again, I tried to establish a foothold. Because the school was small, I was able to play in the high school band. I began as second trumpet behind Rick Patton. God gave me a personality that could not deal with being second. This can be confused with conceit and ego. This is not the case with me.

The reason success in my life was prevalent and accusations of ego and conceit were thrown at me was my desire and attitude that if the time to participate is necessary, I might as well try to be the best. I am a believer that ego and confidence are so closely related that each person's perception will be influenced by their feelings. Experience has taught me that a person's perception of another cannot be controlled. I can encourage search of the truth. How is this done? As written in Samuel, hand it over to Jesus.

Other improvements came too. Though I kept averaging Cs in my schoolwork, I really enjoyed participating in sports. After school, I hung around the gym or ball fields until suppertime. While I was there, the older boys watched out for me. God has blessed me with a personality that is either liked, or disliked. My life is filled with friends. This surprises me because I am forthright, bold, and noisy. I guess the enlarged heart shows. I love my friends, all sizes, shapes, and colors. At one point in my adult life, I was hospitalized, and during that time 113 get well cards were sent to me. One of my friends wanted to know if I owed money to all of them. Most all of my relationships are loaded with teasing and laughter. With this personality the older boys adopted me, so the bullying subsided a bit. Of course, the sand was still shifting. Hard work yielded good results on the basketball court, but all the attention I received wasn't positive.

After a seventh-grade basketball game in Chassell, Michigan, the principal of Chassell High School sent me some pictures he had taken of our game. He complimented my play and asked to take me bowling in a nearby town. I initially thought his subsequent invitation was the ultimate compliment. He had noticed my talents and wanted me to go bowling with him. In the 1950s, his unusual request generated no suspicion. My coaches warned me about accepting gifts while playing sports. The knowledge that gifts could make me ineligible to play sports prompted me to decline the invitation. That refusal was literally a godsend. Within months, this same principal had been arrested for child abuse.

I still liked girls. There was beauty in every one of them. Courage was still an issue, so there were no dates. Having a desire to get attention from the girls, I would try to wear "cool" clothes. One day, Laura Maki gave me a compliment on my shirt. I wore that shirt five days in a row.

There wasn't total failure. In the fifties, the boys team and the cheerleaders routinely shared a bus. During one seventh-grade road trip, I focused on Kathy Rhoades, one year older than me and pretty as could be. I worked up my courage for hours before walking to the back of the bus. I kissed Kathy on the cheek. Now entered the conscience. I wondered if the kiss made me sexually active. I felt guilty more fifties naiveté and innocence.

I have just realized my first two sexual encounters were in a Kindergarten cardboard bus and a seventh-grade school bus. Since I am presently single, I should go for a bus ride. Unfortunately, where I live, the only busses go to Bingo. I am getting to an age where people wear nametags to remember their own name.

GAINING SOME GROUND

With my sex life now in full gear, I wanted girls to notice me, and two kisses were not enough. My father must have recognized the change in me, so he gave me the "sex talk." "Melvin if you ever make a girl pregnant, you will marry her immediately." Pregnant? I had only started my male maturation in the ninth grade and was sure my "gifts" weren't large enough to be a precipitator of babies. I didn't even know how babies came about until I called Jerry Carney, an older friend of our family. We met immediately and I learned about pregnancy. The action didn't sound good to me; after all I was only in the seventh grade. Jerry was a tough street kid. I believed him.

Knowledge didn't help me much then. Between the guilt fostered by my beliefs and the fear instilled by my father, my insecurity was steadfast. My longest relationship before eighteen lasted a meager four months, and I spent two of those four figuring out how to break up without hurting her feelings. I had a life of many girl friends, no girlfriends.

The insecurity continued, but give me a speech, a trumpet, or a ball, and I had no problem. In small, northern Michigan towns, small schools required students to multitask, or athletic teams, bands, and clubs could not exist. I participated in everything. Though my fear and guilt from the past survived,

I developed the drive to become the best at whatever I attempted except in the classroom. The only subject that made any sense to me was history.

My love for sports and God's natural gifts allowed a very successful career, especially in basketball. Not everything was fun. Charley had two sisters in their Junior year of school when I was a freshman. These two girls were very aggressive and protective of Charley. Because of my recognition in basketball I was subject to tremendous harassment from them. I will never forget their names, Betsy and Lisa, another fear. God gave me ways to deal with this very dangerous behavior. I seem to always be positive. Picture this: positive on the outside and scared to death inside. One job was peddling the Grit, a once-a-week newspaper, delivered on Saturdays. My customers called me "the whistling paperboy." Heck, I even whistled in the rain. High school sports annihilated my guilt and fear approach to religion. In 1963, I experienced my first of four divine interventions. I was standing alongside my teammates for the national anthem before a basketball game. A bright light shined on me; and I heard these words: "Lift every room you enter for the rest of your life." Many key people in my life don't believe I am happy every day. The only way I can answer is, "My God asked me to be positive when I was fifteen."

Life goes on, and Jerry Carney wasn't finished making me a man. He wanted to teach me how to handle the bullies by taking me down to the old mine pits and showing me how to box. Jerry never got the chance. Dad found out about my pending lessons and stopped them. Dad said I didn't have to know how to box. "The bigger man just walks away." I finally had my chance to be the bigger man during my junior year, but not exactly the way Dad had counseled me.

We were on Christmas vacation, playing hockey behind the elementary school. The hockey puck was free at mid ice. Roger LeDuc, another school bully, skated toward it. I put my large backside in motion and headed straight for Roger. That puck was going to be mine. For once, I wasn't afraid. I hit Roger as hard as I could. He fell to the ground, dropped his stick, and landed on his wrist, later diagnosed as a sprain. Even shifting sands encounter enough pressure eventually to form the early foundation of sedimentary rock.

My school performance was anything but rock solid. Chemistry was taught by our basketball coach, and he graded on a curve. "Curve." The grading lines looked like a bowling ball in a burlap bag once my grade landed. I cruised through the class with a D-.

French class was different. I liked the teacher, Marc Gauthier, and maybe a French girl was meant for me. Bonjour! Not able to write the language well, I loved speaking the very romantic words. Mr. Gauthier was great, so I signed up for three total years in high school and one semester in college. Forty years later, only karaoke has been added to my portfolio. The junior year in high school was a major turning point in my life. The anxiousness about my physical shortcomings had finally stopped. The fear subsided.

More important to me was our basketball team's 17-4 record in my junior year. My position as point guard and team leader led to many high school awards and team friendships that continue today. When I graduated from high school, White Pine was inhabited by white-collar families residing in nearly identical mining town houses and leading synonymous lives. These families, nourished by the fathers' ability to provide, expected their children to excel. In our class of twenty, all went on to be successful in life. I went on to college.

I had a different kind of education before my college career commenced. The Hazel Park Raceway boys—uncles Hugo, Alphonse, and Tohn-made sure of that. I worked in Detroit during the summers. Hugo helped me celebrate my twenty-first birthday, Alphonse moved to Florida and taught me how to bet Jai Alai, and John and I frequented local pool halls to garnish up a wager. I sure learned how to have fun. Of course fiscal responsibility sat on the sidelines, as I never quite figured out why my money was all gone after one of our get-togethers.

MUDSLIDE

Summers always ended quickly, and it was time to choose a college. The decision to attend Northern Michigan University was difficult because of basketball. Several Division II colleges wanted me to play ball for them, but my parents wanted me to study in college and felt that playing basketball would hurt my grades. I loved the game and, in retrospect, would probably have taken advantage of the opportunity to play if my parents had supported that choice. NMU offered a good music program, so I chose to go there. I would enroll two weeks before school to attend marching band practice. As my parents drove off, I stood on the sidewalk near Gries Hall in my black suit, black shoes, and brand-new white socks. Believe me, the socks made the outfit.

My new home, Gries Hall, was the athletic dormitory, and the football players were also on campus early. Dave Peterson, Mike Baxter, and I were the only band students in the football players' dorm. Within three days, the three of us musicians were doing the seniors' chores and wearing freshman beanies. Those players were so big that I would have worn pampers if they had demanded it.

Fortunately, Bill Sanderson and two other quarterbacks were our suitemates. Quarterbacks were a bit more sophisticated than the three-hundred-pound linemen, who never showered and threw food at each other. Eventually, Dave and Mike turned out to be an asset to the football players, as they tutored some of the team. Once the players saw my high school grades, I was appointed the pizza deliveryman.

During the first day of band practice, I didn't fare much better. In my audition with Dr. Loren Richtmeyer, I was asked to play "The Ticonderoga March." I drew my instrument to my lips and played a song I had never heard of. I played loud and felt confident. Dr. Richtmeyer said that my tone was good but I had played the song in B flat rather than the requisite B sharp. I had no idea how to read a musical score with five sharps. I played trumpet by ear, and B flat was the only key I knew. By the time I left the room, I figured I'd be demoted to the *oom pah pahs* I had started with in seventh grade. Dr. Richtmeyer surprised me by seating me thirteenth (of fourteen) first chairs and telling me to learn the correct notes.

Signing up for classes went well too. My advisor signed me up for sixteen credits, the maximum allowed for freshmen. I would major in physical education and history and was quite sure I could handle this load. After all, I only had three hours of class per day, band practice in the afternoon, and the entire evening off. What a life! I thought I'd have plenty of time for a job in the Wildcat Den, a small food court where I would sweep, mop, and cook in emergencies. The first week went quite well. I easily handled all three commitments. But college life was different: no rules, no parents, and no guilt when one lived that far from home. I had a free pass, and I took full advantage of it.

During my first Friday night, I met old PBR, Pabst Blue Ribbon, the drink of choice. Lucky Strikes were the beer chaser. I rolled the cigarettes in the arm of my t-shirt, held the beer in my right hand, and "shackled" my pants (lowered the waist). Hair was combed in a duck's ass, cigarette hung off the lower lip, and the total package was ready for an evening out. This became routine for Friday nights. I even developed a tolerance for both the cigarettes and the liquor.

Joyce Shaftner, a beautiful young woman from White Pine, asked me to go to Lansing, Michigan, for the weekend with her. I couldn't stop shaking. The specter of pregnancy, and perhaps some of my old church guilt, made me decline. Fear that my parents might find out forced me to decline not only Joyce but also Mary, Barb, Becky, and others during that freshman year.

I started missing my 8:00 a.m. class. After all, it was just geography—dirt and rocks. How hard could a, b, c, or d exams be? Besides, Dr. Roine didn't take attendance. All of my classes became a blur. My studying was done in a sauna on Third Street. My refreshment was a jumbo of beer. I was too young to drink in the bars. Once I was old enough, I took masters classes at Andy's Bar. I drank so much that I could have become a liquor inspector. Academic probation loomed in my future. I had one semester to get my grades up to avoid expulsion. Of course, Dad wasn't happy. I had to repeat all of the first semester classes.

The college honeymoon was over. I was missing the security of home, so I started hitchhiking to White Pine every other weekend. I felt more secure there.

When the second semester began, I found out that questions on tests were not so foreign to me. My favorite exams were multiple choice. I had a 25 percent chance of answering correct. Lots of hard work garnered me a respectable C+ GPA in that semester, which allowed me to return in the fall for my second year. I was still on academic probation.

During our two-week vacation for Christmas in 1965, some friends and I attended a high school basketball game. Everyone knew me because of my basketball days, so I didn't walk-I swaggered. I had the mouth, the aggressiveness, and the desire, so I started looking for girls. I mean just because I hadn't taken advantage of my opportunities with women up to this point didn't mean I lacked interest. After all, the subject was forever to my mind.

A good candidate caught my eye. Buxom and pretty, Margaret Harrison sat in the stands with one of her friends. My three friends and I circled the two girls, and we garnered enough interest to warrant some considerable time with them. By the end of the game, my friends and I had convinced the delectable Margaret and her friend to allow us to escort them home. Once we arrived, Joe read a comic book, Mark watched television, and Charley talked to the friend. Margaret chose me. That evening offered every opportunity I ever dreamed of. It ended with some foreplay and a good night kiss. I could not participate. This time my conscience saved my life.

Two days later, the Gogebic County police car, accompanied by Charley, Joe, and Mark, was parked in my parents' driveway. The sheriff delivered a warrant for my arrest for the statutory rape of one Miss Margaret Harrison.

We had a forty-five-minute trip to the jail in Gogebic County. The four of us turned in our valuables, posed for our mug shots, and were fingerprinted. A judge set bail for $1,000 for all of us. It was Sunday. We had to stay overnight in jail.

The sheriff separated the four of us. My three friends rated private cells. I shared a cell with eleven people of Indian heritage from the same town of Iron River, where the game was played. My bed was five feet wide. The sink had no faucets, and bathroom privileges were not private. Within several hours, my parents visited.

My father and mother met me in a private room. Dad looked seven feet tall. I thanked God that I wasn't guilty when my dad asked, "Did you do it? If you did, you will rot in jail. If you didn't, I will sell my house to set you free."

Bail was arranged for Monday afternoon. That day and a half in jail will never be forgotten. I learned how to play Solitaire, but mostly, I cried and vomited. The four of us were happy to return home in wait for a day in court.

Our attorney, Marvin Santori, didn't finalize our case until late February. During this time, the "jail birds" were not allowed to date our classmates. Parents were not sure of our innocence.

To help facilitate an end to this mudslide, we requested a lie detector test for everyone, including Ms. Harrison. The state police called me at college early in February. The test would be taken in Marquette, where I was attending school. The officer offered to send a car to pick me up. Just what I needed in front of my college dormitory—a police escort. I declined the offer. I would make my own arrangements.

At police headquarters, we were separated. We couldn't communicate before the test. Mark was first, Charley second, and me third. I sat in a large chair with bands on my hands, wrist, arm, and chest in front of the one-way window you always see on television. The officer fired abrupt questions at me and told me to simply answer yes or no. When I had completed the test, the officer looked at me and yelled, "You are lying. Tell the truth." Terrified and crying, I begged for a retest.

Finally released, I met up with Charley and Mark. They repeated my experience with the tester, Apparently, the accusations were a ruse to catch the guilty. When Joe finished, we asked about his experience. He said, "I told him to shove the machine up his ass. I was reading a comic book."

With God's direction, we not only passed the test but departed this horrific situation with what I believe was a divine intervention. Someone with less faith would credit an attorney in the law offices of Sartori, Mackay, and James. Attorney James had a chance to review our case and remembered the name Harrison. "Harrison, Margaret Harrison?" he said to his partner. "Let me make a phone call." James had formerly practiced in Seattle, Washington, and remembered a statutory rape case involving a Washington man and a Margaret Harrison from Iron River, Michigan. It was the same person, and all charges were dropped.

The lie detector tests established our innocence and revealed no clear conclusion regarding Margaret, whom the tester described as confused. She subsequently dropped the charges. It was 1966.

SPROUTING

I officially earned my BS degree and took a teaching job at St. Michael's Catholic School in Marquette-just a few blocks from the university, It was another blessing to find a job in the winter of 1970.

Teaching in a parochial school was an eye-opener for me. We would start the day with church, where the mass ended with the offering. We also took an offering in the Lutheran church, but the Catholics had their basket on a long stick. It looked like a fishing pole.

All students wore uniforms, and the girls used to roll their skirts above their knees when the parents were not around. I sure am glad that I was twenty-two when I taught there because we had one bathroom time at 2:30 in the afternoon. If I were teaching there today, I would have to wear Depends.

While teaching at St. Michaels, I was asked to coach' junior high basketball at John D. Pierce, located across the street. That coaching position lead to a freshman basketball position in the fall of 1969 while student teaching at Ishpeming High School, just seventeen miles west of Marquette.

Ishpeming had over fifty young men try out for a team that carried fifteen players. One young man who did not make the top fifteen was Kyle Ranken. I thought enough of Kyle to keep him around as team manager. I hurt Kyle badly when he was released; and forty years later, I am a scar in this man's life. At the age of twenty-one, I had no idea what empathy was. Kyle loved basketball as much as I did. A twenty-one-year-old coach shattered his dreams of having a basketball career. As the problem with the Law scarred me, not allowing Kyle the right to play basketball is a permanent scar for him.

I learned a couple of important lessons. Freshman can grow by leaps and bounds. Kyle later chose to participate in intramural basketball. He not only had grown but developed his basketball skills and became one of the top players in the intramural league. People in leadership positions can do a lot of unintentional harm to young people. Because of Kyle Ranken, I never cut student athletes in any sport for ten years, the extent of my teaching and coaching.

While teaching and coaching at St. Michaels, John D. Pierce, and Ishpeming, I earned my bachelors degree and would pursue a full-time teaching position. I would graduate in January of 1970 with a degree in education. In the summer of 1969 I married my first wife, Julie. Julie worked at the university and would continue until graduation. Julie is a beautiful woman, resembles Sophia Loren in her glorious years. Her family was, and still is, great. I still am Uncle Mel to many of the children. Being the so-called high school star, I was used to getting my way. Not with Julie. That was very attractive to me; the chase was something new. This young woman was loaded with looks, brains, and ability. Her family was beautiful. We married.

Full-time teaching positions in northern Michigan were not available, so my wife and I interviewed in the Lower Peninsula. Morrice High School, just outside of Lansing, Michigan's capitol, was first. After the interview, my wife and I had mixed emotions about that position. That afternoon,

I interviewed for a history/physical education position in a consolidated high school comprised of Vermontville and Nashville. Also included were assistant coaching positions in football and basketball. I had lots of basketball experience. Football would be an entirely new challenge.

The prinicipal, Joe Winston, had seven Upper Peninsula (northern Michigan) teachers on staff. Mr. Winston liked teachers who controlled their classrooms, and that was a behavior learned from our upbringing. He offered me the position. At age twenty-two, my wife and I would move seven and one half hours away from home and family.

Though I was only four years older than the seniors I was teaching, I remembered the advice from a teacher at White Pine: "Be tough on your students for the first two weeks. Once they understand who controls the classroom, you can always develop calmer relationships. Some students will challenge a new teacher."

A nineteen-year-old senior boy walked by me in the hallway and said, "This young, punk teacher has to go." I asked a fellow teacher what I should do. He told me I had no boundaries. Three days later, I pushed Daryl up against the locker, challenged him, and hauled him off to the principal's office. When Principal Winston supported me, Daryl never challenged me again. Of course, you realize that in 1970, this action was not acceptable. If the same incident occurred today, I would be back playing Solitaire in jail for abuse.

One other student/athlete challenged me during my Maple Valley tenure. A junior varsity basketball player's behavior needed addressing. With little remorse from the young man, I suspended him for one game. His father contacted the board of education to challenge my decision. The board understood my reasoning and gave me their unanimous support.

In my fourth year, I added coaching the varsity track team to my schedule of basketball and football, I now made $9,400 per year, a long way from the $5,900 at St. Michaels. In the '70's $10,000 per year was my goal.

As the '70's were coming to a close, the income never seemed to be enough. Teachers started to lose their autonomy in the classroom. I was becoming restless.

SLIPPERY SLOPE

Not all the decisions I made in those years were good ones. I knew the day I married my first wife, Julie, that I was not in love. It wasn't Julie's fault, and I knew better. Looking for a great life surrounded by nice people, I was attracted to Julie and to her beautiful family. I figured I could help Julie realize her great attributes. We could make love legally and live happily ever after. Wasn't that what grown-ups did?

Julie and I stayed together for twenty years, and the best part of those twenty years is our two daughters. Children are angels in progress, the most blessed creation that two people can produce. Exciting and wonderful from conception to birth, our first gift was born in December of 1970. For nine months, we watched the growth and development of our first beautiful baby girl, whom we named Amy Grace.

Growing up in conservative northern Michigan, the son of religious parents, I had no idea what to expect in the birth process. My first shock came when the nurses asked me to go to a waiting room since they needed to shave my wife. "Shave what?" My return to her room wasn't much better. When I saw my wife's expressions and heard her discomfort during the birth process, I empathized way too much. I had frequent labor pains too and often rang the buzzer to summon nurses to my wife's aid. Everyone told me my reaction was normal, but I now know it was symptomatic of a problem I would struggle with throughout my life—not labor pains, caring too much.

I had all kinds of questions about being a father. Being a new parent is scary. I knew Julie and I needed to be responsible parents and that we needed a system of discipline and behavior. I don't think I asked Julie; I just decided, from the outset, that we would use tough love, a consistent system of respect and accountability, to raise our daughter. Her world would be full of positive reinforcement. "Shoot for the moon," I would tell her. "If you miss, you will still be a star." I would tell her every day that she was beautiful. I would make sure she had every opportunity. Nothing could stop us.

Julie, Amy, and I settled in Charlotte, Michigan. We worshipped together at the Peace Lutheran Church. Monday through Friday, I drove the twenty miles to and from Charlotte to Maple Valley High School. The length of my days and the distance didn't work out well for Julie, so we moved to Vermontville, much closer to the school. If Julie needed me, I could get home quickly.

Two years later, Julie was expecting again. I was back in that same waiting room, but this time, there was little time. Our second little angel, Cory Ann, arrived. I thought this situation was wonderful. When I stood up to go to Julie's room to see my new daughter, the nurse told me that Julie didn't want to see me. She was suffering from a condition the nurse called blue Monday. "Blue Monday? What?" My heart sank to my shoes. Julie and I hadn't been getting along very well, but I couldn't have guessed that she would deny me access to my new daughter.

Now the empathy leads to codependence. I did not yet understand that a person can help too much, that a person can hinder another's development by doing too much. I learned that anything done to excess usually has low success. I tried everything I knew to please my wife—including staying away physically when she wanted me to. I really didn't know what to do. We were a young married couple, sleeping together, yet alone.

Our personal life was kept private where, in public, we acted like a model couple. Amy became my mascot cheerleader during the high school basketball games. Julie and Cory watch from the stands. Everything seemed fine on the surface. I coached track and football as well. Amy rode the track bus with me, and I knew that pretty Amy was going to be very special; she already had a winning personality and lots of confidence. Cory, like Amy, was gorgeous and developing her own special personality.

We completed the idyllic family portrait when we bought our first home in Nashville, Michigan—a spot even closer to the Maple Valley School. Cliché though it maybe, a house doesn't make a home. We were about to crash land at the bottom of a mountain of negativity built over the previous four years.

AVALANCHE

Julie and I lost whatever was left of our relationship in 1974. I had an empty stomach, growling both for answers and for some nurturing. When I finally confronted her, I was told that she did not love me and wanted to take Amy and Cory to Rochester, New York, to live with her sister, Rhonda. She had been contacting Jay Hinkson, a former acquaintance from Norther Michigan University.

Totally devastated, I drove over to Peace Lutheran Church in Charlotte to seek counsel with pastor Wayne Strohshein. After several counseling sessions, Pastor Wayne told me that, Julie's leaving was not a problem for me. The real problem was that she—not I—had made the decision. It was an ego thing. I wasn't happy; neither was she. But she made the decision to end our marriage, not me.

The move to dissolve our marriage did not happen overnight. We didn't fight. I was resigned to being single again and began making arrangements to travel to New York once a month to see my precious daughters. Because the girls were still young—just four and two—I would be able to see them during the school year and share time during the summers. After four months, we sold the house, realigned insurance policies to match our new status, and made the necessary arrangements for a U-Haul truck, which we would drive to

New York. We were determined to make this separation as painless as possible for the girls.

Numb and resolute, I managed the trip fairly well. We headed for Detroit, Michigan, where we would cross the Canadian border and travel to Niagra Falls, New York. The four of us and all of our belongings filled the largest U-Haul we could find. When I pulled up to US Customs to re-enter United States from Canada, the border agent insisted on opening the hatch of the U-Haul. We were not allowed to bring plants across the border, and I would have to unload the entire U-Haul. Instead of getting flustered, I became a salesman—a nomenclature that would remain with me for decades. I painted a visual of our family's current trauma, and the border guard decided to let us through.

Four hours later, we reached Auntie Rhonda and Rochester, New York. After greeting her sister, I sat at The kitchen table with Julie and made sure the insurance coverage, financial support, and visitation times were all in order. I gave Amy and Cory big hugs, grabbed a cup of coffee, and jumped into my brother-in-law's car. He was taking me to the airport to fly back to Michigan. Until I was in the car, I was stoic. I didn't want to upset Amy and Cory. The stoicism quickly disappeared once I was alone. I cried.

Returning to my town did little to assuage my sorrow. I had nowhere to live, and my financial page looked pretty ugly. I began a long, sad journey to rebuild a life without my two little girls. I can't even express my lonely dissolution. Only those who have lived it can truly understand. A fellow employee of Maple Valley solved one problem. Harry Bancroft was a custodian and a close friend with a vacant mobile home on Lake Hastings just fifteen miles from the high school. I could use the home free of charge. In a word, it was perfect.

Even though I continued to miss my daughters, living alone was not difficult for me. I was ready to date again; actually, the possibilities excited me. I would fly to New York once a month to spend some time with my daughters. Everything was falling into place.

Julie and I had never told our families about the separation. I flew into Ironwood (upper Michigan) and met Mom at the airport. During our drive to White Pine, I told her all the details of my new living arrangements and explained how Julie and I had handled our freefall. Mom was concerned about me—my welfare—and Amy and Cory's future. I reassured her about my commitment to honor all responsibilities. Telling Mom was easy. If I ran over her with my car, she would still insist I was a good driver.

Telling Dad was very different. He immediately queried, "What's going on?" Parents have intuition about their children, and I was convinced Dad knew something was wrong. The problem was that he didn't really want to know what that something was. After I told him, he quickly responded, "Why are you telling us? You're going to make our marriage miserable!" Despite the apparent egocentrism, Dad was really a caring man. He simply wanted a private and peaceful life and had treated me the same way he would treat any other adult. He apologized once he calmed down and asked if he could help. "Seeing the girls is crucial," I told him. He agreed and offered to pay half of my plane fare for my monthly trips to Syracuse.

After visiting with my parents, I headed to Ishpeming to tell Julie's mother. Her dad had passed away years before. She was drying dishes and putting them in the cupboard when I delivered my news. She never stopped working, never blinked an eye, though disappointment painted her face. Like my parents, she was concerned about Amy and Cory but accepted Julie's and my visitation schedule.

DIGGING OUT

One month passed quickly. I would often search the sky, look out the clouds, and picture my little girls sitting up there. I prayed I would be able to see them. My answer came but not in the way I had expected.

I was organizing some games in my physical education class when a Michigan State policeman drove up and asked to see Mr. Ruohonen. Terrified that something had happened to Amy and Cory, I searched the officer's face. My terror frenzy had been unnecessary. This officer, my cousin, was on his way to Lansing, the state capital, to deliver the grapes from his vineyard. I would soon experience a more important delivery: my girls.

Julie wanted to come home. I felt ambivalent. I was excited to bring my girls home but terrified about Julie re-entering my life. The girls were too important, I decided. I had to take a chance. Flying to New York just one month after I had left, I made arrangements for another U-Haul to return our belongings and family to Hastings, Michigan. We drove through the United States this time to void customs.

I was jubilant. It was fall, the leaves adorned the Land, and my friend Harry's pontoon boat was sitting in full view, just waiting to be used. More importantly, Amy, Cory, Julie, and I were a family again. I rented a motorcycle from one of my former football players and dressed like an Eskimo to stay warm for the twenty-mile excursion each day to school. That sacrifice was well worth it. Julie, Amy, and Cory had use of the vehicle during the day. Julie was extremely attentive to me. Our relationship was wonderful, and I was happy. We decided to rent a little brown house near the Maple Valley school. This house had a big backyard surrounded by cornfields. We purchased a female black lab named Hogan. Everything seemed perfect, the proverbial calm before the storm.

After six months, our relationship returned to our more common marital schemata—isolation, discord, and neglect. I kept busy with teaching, coaching, and bowling in a league on Wednesday nights. One Wednesday changed my life. In 1979, one my football assistants commented on my ability to entertain twenty eight lanes of bowlers and make them laugh. Ricky told me, "You missed your calling. Get into sales and make big bucks." He also wanted to switch coaching positions. I would be head junior varsity football coach and he the assistant. Fifty-four young men tried out for the football team—forty-one more than the previous year Coach Ricky reiterated my career decision.

Convinced that Ricky might have a point, I contacted Northern Michigan University's placement director—the same man who had been instrumental In garnering my Maple Valley job. I told Mr. Harmon I wanted to leave teaching and get a job in sales, marketing, and public relations. After all, I had a degree in history, health, and physical education—a perfect match. He laughed and told me the transition I wanted was highly unlikely.

A short time later, Julie, Amy, Cory, and I were headed for a day at a Lake Michigan beach during Labor Day weekend when Julie asked if I had listened to the phone message from

NMU. Apparently, Mr. Harmon wanted to talk to me. Since it was a Friday afternoon and the beginning of a long weekend, I stopped at a pay phone to call him. He told me a company called the Mid-America Corporation, was looking for two Representatives to sell insurance, but he assured me that Mid-America was worth looking into.

I took his advice and set up a meeting at Sambo's Restaurant in East Lansing. Mid-America's sales manager, Nick Thompson, met me there and indicated there were two open positions: one in Traverse City and one in Marquette, Michigan. My eyes opened wide when he offered me a salary equal to all ten previous years of teaching, plus commission, an expense account, and a brand-new Caprice Classic. Because I was a Yooper, he thought the Marquette position would be better, and he'd let me know in a few days.

On Sunday evening—just two days later—Mr. Thompson offered me the Marquette position. Mid-America would pay all the moving expenses. I would work for two weeks in Saginaw, Michigan, a daily four hour round trip.

Julie drove me the first day. I drove my new car home that evening. We needed to update my clothes, so I bought a used sport coat for fifty dollars. Mr. Thompson laughed when he opened the lapel and found "J.C. Pinaa." a Penny's brand. I figured his suit had been previously owned by three people, as his lapel read "Hart-Shaffner and Marx."

To contribute to the sliding of our marriage. I don't remember discussing this move with Julie. I was a driven person, and the move would be good for our family. Later in life, I learned that I always listened well. The question was, Did I hear? Listening precipitated action. Hearing would have dissuaded me from trying to be life's savior. That lesson finally sunk in when I was sixty-two. Now, when I listen, I hear. I finally "get it."

What I didn't get was the idea that a firm would hire a mover to pack, load, and haul all of our personal belongings across the Mackinaw Bridge to our new home. We felt so guilty that we rented a U-Haul, packed it ourselves, and had our nephew drive our car and follow the U-Haul. The Mid-America Corporation must have laughed about our naïveté. Of course, we couldn't leave Maple Valley until we tied up some loose ends. I wrote my letter of resignation, a healthy combination of, "Thanks for Everything," and, "Take this job and shove it." Parents of Maple Valley hosted six parties for me. Peace Lutheran also celebrated my departure with a party. People teased me that everyone was so happy I was leaving they wanted to celebrate. It was a special time. Twenty-eight years later, I'm not so glib. Now I believe that one should never take down a fence until he knows why it was put up in the first place. We moved in October of 1979.

Our move north encountered a snowstorm, which made an eight-hour trip last fourteen hours. We arrived in Ispeming, Michigan, with a foot of snow on the ground. The most important thing was that we were all safe. We were near Julie's family again, joined Bethany Lutheran Church, and settled in to the community where we had married ten years and a couple Lifetimes before.

Our daughters grew up in Ishpeming. Amy, the oldest, was aggressive like me. She would try anything from talent contests to cheerleading. She led an interesting life, drawing attention from all segments. Cory really did well, despite having such a talented sister to follow. The "tough love" approach to raise the girls continued. Speaking honestly, I don't feel comfortable with any other way to teach. In my sixty-two years, I feel that people who are responsible and accountable for their behavior excel in life. The downfall to this approach is the recipient rarely feels the power of the love. Our society seems to accept the softer approach, like sand moving in a light breeze.

FLOUNDERING ONCE AGAIN

I didn't have much luck with family relationships during this time, but I certainly knew how to make money. Money came in so often and in such large amounts that I started to resent my wife. Julie had the best clothes, drove a Cadillac, and joined the Country Club. Amy and Cory were so busy that I purchased a car for each. No one ever asked how I made the money, so I never told them. One month I made $27,000. I almost had a nervous breakdown. I drove to Houghton and purchased a television, antenna, and who knows what else for my parents. I secretly paid college fees so a niece could complete nursing school. Why? Money never brought happiness. I wanted a love relationship, and that wasn't happening.

Sure, we had positive moments, but they were always the result of a new purchase. Money bought temporary happiness.

I wasn't obvious to the "add booze and you lose" adage. I was lonely and unhappy. I needed an escape, and alcohol worked. Money also caused me pain. At the golf course, I always had a thousand dollars in my wallet. I used some of that to help a "friend," a hardworking teacher with three boys in college. I played him in golf, even though I knew he was a better golfer. I figured my family didn't deserve any more cash. The money served his family better. Our contests garnered extra cash for him every week. I eventually found out that Arnold was playing me, duping me into betting more and more on different holes. Others were laughing at me behind my back. The games stopped when I learned what was going on. The hurt stays.

My actions invited someone to take advantage of me. Your foundation will stop shifting when you accept that an action causes a reaction. C. Peter Marshall Encourages discernment. I did not know what discernment really meant, nor did I use the term. Reflecting back to this time in the 80's, I trusted everyone, always, looked for the good in people, and was oblivious to anyone intentionally trying to hurt me. I also feel all I thought about was how hard this man worked for so little money. All I had to do was talk and be honest and money came in all directions. I guess my feeling would be one of empathy. That surface discernment of my golfing friend ended in disappointment and pain.

On the surface I should blame Arnold. That behavior would cause a "shifting sand" relationship. To crystallize this situation I had to take responsibility for my participation in the golf matches. This part of my personality stayed with me to age sixty. I would always go overboard with everything in my life. I over trust, over empathize, and take co-dependency to the maximum. I did this with my wives and, mostly, my daughters. There is not a day that goes by where I don't think of my daughters.

My choice to require my daughters to take responsibility for their actions and to encourage independence has its ramifications. I am a firm believer that tough love is the best path to a life built on a rock. The pitfall seems to be a lack of recognition of love. There is no person or any behavior that can stop my feelings for and to Amy and Cory. One must look below the surface to see it with people who harbored deceitful aspirations. Be accountable for your shortcomings and responsible for your actions.

The downward emotional cycle tends to propagate itself. One night, in a local restaurant/lounge, I encountered a younger friend whom I had known since Maple Valley teaching days. I was friends with his uncle when Donny joined our fishing expeditions in Canada. At an all-time low in my life, I was searching for a life raft. Donny told me he had been working for a commercial cleaning company but really wanted to start his own business. Within two weeks, we started All Seasons Cleaning Service. I borrowed $19,000 from a local bank, and All Seasons Cleaning Service was up and running.

This decision was purely emotional, and I became an absentee owner. My focus was on insurance and my failing marriage. Leaving Donny alone to supervise people and to market our product was not fair to him. Subsequently our retail sales fell, forcing Donny to leave to support his family.

A friend offered to buy All Seasons Cleaning. I had to own up to total ignorance as to the financial condition, or value of equipment and customer base. The only solution was to send the potential owner, Bruce, to a local banker trusted by both of us. They were to come with a fair price, one that I had no reason to question for very irresponsible reasons of not paying attention to the operations. Again, no fault to Bruce, it was too late to save the business.

Money was still flowing in my personal operations. I really liked Bruce and gave him an opportunity to join me marketing products to banks and auto dealers. It was an easy transition for Bruce as he knew my excellent secretary Nora. I owned my own insurance brokerage and made a name change from a subsidiary of the Mid-America Life Corporation to First Initiative, Inc. This happened in the mid-90's.

Hiring Bruce and having Nora as secretary seemed to be a perfect team. My two employees were closer than I thought. Michigan's economy slowed down, as did our account base. Adjustments had to be made. I reduced the size of my office. Bruce wanted more responsibility, but not in the way I had intended. He told me that he was leaving, that he my secretary had orchestrated a deal with a competitor. They would now sell insurance and compete for my bank and auto portfolio.

As mentioned in the beginning of the book, my father was very emphatic to never lie, cheat, or steal. I am proud to say I have lived up to his teachings, and because of that I had great customer relationships. My accounts did not tolerate Bruce and Nora's attempt to capture my business. As my accounts stayed loyal, resentment formed between the three of us. Threats were made against me, which are still on record at the county sheriff's office. Nothing has occurred to this date; all is forgiven on my part. The only effect this had on me was sadness. Nora is a fantastic person, and Bruce was my golf partner, card playing partner, and friend. I would let both back in my life tomorrow. I really enjoy the act of forgiveness. I am so thankful I have been forgiven by most people. My personality can err. I am a busy person.

GATHERING SEDIMENT

Interest rates rose to 20 percent in the early eighties. Home and auto loans were at a minimum. Since my business centered on loans, our family lived modestly for two years. In 1982, I approached Howard Kolhoff, President of the Mid-America Corporation, and proposed a change in my income from salary to straight commission. He agreed. I was scared as I had been when I left my teaching position. I narrowly avoided panic attacks when I thought about the difficulty of life on commission. The choice turned out to be a good one for me.

In my third year on commission, my income rose from an average of $78,000 per year to $152,000. Then it rose from $152,000 to $174,000. One year, when Reagan took office, it was $227,000. But no amount of money can bring true happiness if life has no foundation. A passage in Samuel I encourages believers to ask God where your donkeys are, never to chase your donkeys. My interpretation is found in I Samuel, chapter 9. Please do not be too critical as I really was caught up on the donkeys.

What I really mean is to gather all the facts relating to your concern and turn them over to Jesus in prayer. I find this very comforting. As related in The Shack, a person doesn't have to become over zealous to stop Living, learn to relax, forgive, enjoy our frailties, and "smell the roses." I was living such a fast life during this period that I didn't ask about my donkeys. I knew they were in bars, Vegas, travel, and excitement. I had no home life, so I filled the empty spaces with new people and new places. The unfortunate part of this lifestyle is that I passed in on to my daughters. I wasn't living on shifting sand; I was engulfed in a landslide.

I would choose this period of time as the most difficult with my first family. My psyche was so fragile that I hardly remember how Julie and the girls were doing, something I regret. My doctor told me that I was heading for a stroke and would have one if I didn't do something about my marriage. My blood pressure skyrocketed. My cholesterol was high. Most destructive was a combination of depression and anxiety. These conditions prompted our family to see a psychologist. Amy and Cory went once. Julie went several times before the three of them decided they wouldn't return. I continued as I was—and continue to be—interested in learning about myself. One thing I did learn is that trying to do good isn't always enough. Another is that running fastest means you are always alone.

I won't even venture to grade myself with Amy and Cory. There are so many things I would do differently if I was an experienced father. They had reason to question my technique but never my love.

Julie was a different story. We were living in a new low. Neither Julie nor I were happy. My conscience wouldn't allow infidelity. That would be like toting a Derringer during a world war. Lust was different though. I filled my needs without cheating by spending time in groups of younger people or people in my age group who thought young. Any chance I had, I went where these people were. My insides were imploding, but my outside was enjoying.

I will never blame Julie for the failure of our marriage. My dominant personality contributed much to our demise and never allowed Julie the chance to develop. I didn't feel the love necessary for a successful union. Everything I did was based on guilt, the church, and what the neighbors thought.

I experienced a third divine intervention at home. During one of our marriage lows I was sitting in my basement office when a strong message came via the same bright light in the two previous directives. "Go! You have done enough in your marriage. I am truly convinced a person has to watch for the messages from above. I, very seldom, hope for anything anymore. When something happens today, I immediately think it must not have been good for me. I have learned to only give my love to people or things that can return love. This pretty much eliminates material possessions.

My twenty-year marriage was over, and I searched for the least painful path through this terrible ordeal. I visited the school guidance counselor to solicit some advice. I asked her to watch over Amy and Cory once they found out I was leaving. Then, I went home to tell Julie. I would take my clothes out of the house and move to the Holiday Inn in Marquette until I could find something more permanent. The girls would have to choose where they wanted to live. Cory, sixteen, moved in with me. Amy, eighteen, stayed at home with Mom.

With no available apartments to rent, the search became difficult. One of my friends, on an overnight decision, moved out of his place at Tourville Apartments. Those apartments were my first choice. Only one set of footprints again.

Julie and I retained attorneys, and as any Library Book with the subject heading "divorce" will tell you, we moved quickly through the common stages: understanding, tears, hatred, and finally, combat. The only material possession I wanted was the cabin. Julie was well aware of that, but I didn't argue when she said the first possession she wanted was the cabin. Alimony was mandatory. Julie was entitled to enough money to sustain the lifestyle to which she was accustomed. I had two options: pay alimony until I was sixty-six or pay huge sums for three years and be done. I chose the latter, a poor decision that continues to harangue me today.

During the next four years, I was in a high state of oblivion with a fast social life and alcohol. On this path of destruction, I was too numb to know the impact this behavior was having on my loved ones. The only eraser for my poor decisions is forgiveness, and God was working overtime with me.

TAIL LIGHTS OVER THE HILL

From 1988 until 1991, Cory and I lived in Marquette. I lived responsibly during the day and partied all night. I dated many women, fell in love for two weeks at a time, and then moved on to another. That was my life. My friend, known to us as Fast Freddie, called my apartment the wonder room—wonder who has been over lately. I was drinking so much that I have difficulty remembering names, but I do remember I had many great ladies in my life. I get embarrassed when I think about them because I was an irresponsible drunk when they knew me. If only they could see me now. Actually, I would honestly like another chance with some of them. At this point in my life it was the late 1980's. Cory was living with me and driving fifteen miles to high school each day. I have been asked many times how Cory was dealing with this separation from her mom. I don't know. Writing this book is the first time thinking about what Cory and Amy were going through. This does not make me feel very good.

Three years of alimony passed in a surface relationship/booze blur. I scheduled a Renaissance party at the Shamrock Bar in Marquette after the last alimony payment. Invitations were mailed. Freddie; his wife, Julia; and I went to a local bar to deliver invitations. While we were at J.T. Shifts, I saw a young lady I had dated several times before. She was sitting with a beautiful blonde who looked a lot like Lorrie Morgan, the country singer. Fast Freddie earned his nomenclature that night. Before I knew it, that beautiful girl, sixteen years my junior, was sitting in my car with Fred, his wife, and me. We were off to the Shamrock to practice for the party. On party night, Angie was invited to join me. We celebrated by sharing gifts, singing karaoke, and drinking $971.00 worth of booze.

Prior to meeting Angie in 1990, I wasn't able to earn enough money to pay alimony and maintain my business. I chose not to pay the IRS. That was a terrible decision. My CPA was against that decision, but I am hard headed and didn't listen. After my divorce settlement was honored, I would set up a payment program to pay the back taxes.

To prepare for the IRS, I purchased every book telling me of my rights. When my CPA and I would meet with IRS officer Larry Komstadt, I would be organized. I had prepared a budget with financial statements and a plan. Unfortunately, it doesn't work that way. Larry wanted my church donations deleted from the plan. I sat up in my chair and said, "If I can't give to the church, I won't go to work. I work on straight commission. And if the church doesn't get any money, neither will you. Furthermore, if the IRS won't work with me, I'll take the IRS to Connie Chung and CBS News." Imagine my chagrin when Tom, my CPA, informed me that CBS had fired Ms. Chung. After a short deliberation, the church offering was allowed. I will be paying back taxes until 2014.

That wasn't the only deal I was working on. Angie moved into my apartment. She was very proud of her new mobile home, so I purchased lake property forty-five miles from Marquette. We move her mobile home to the lake. At the time, she was twenty-eight and I was forty-four.

Angie had a six-year-old son named Barry. Living together, not married, was very uncomfortable for me. My parents visited us once at my apartment. My father asked, "Where does Angie sleep?" I wanted to tell him that she slept in the bed and I slept standing up. The Old Lutheran upbringing flashed in front of me. I was on my way to hell—do not pass go, do not collect $200; just go straight to hell.

Angie and I later moved from the Tourville apartments to a house on Oak Street five miles outside of town. On one Sunday afternoon, we purchased a beautiful white Eskimo Pup named Misty.

Life was great. We travelled to Cancun, Key West, and all over the United States. After five years together, Angie suggested we marry. I insisted that everything be top shelf. We would marry at Messiah Lutheran Church in Marquette and host a gigantic reception at the Ramada Inn. Many would be invited to share in our special day.

Our marriage was wonderful for two years. We enjoyed the same things, and money was plentiful. I don't think we were ever in love, just in lust. Our life together from 1990 to 1996 was one big party. For instance, in 1991, I met a group of golfers in Gaylord, Michigan, for a four-day golf and drinking tour. Drinking and driving was the norm; never once did we fear getting caught. On our last night in Gaylord, the entire gang was celebrating at the Holiday Inn. The lights blinked. That indicated one of two things: we had either drunk all of their booze, or it was closing time. It was time to leave the bar. Everyone was hungry, so I became the designated driver.

We were off to Mary's Restaurant for a 2:30 a.m. breakfast. That's the only part of the new day that went well. On the way back to our motel, Officer Smith, Gaylord City policeman, followed my car into the motel parking lot. When I opened my car door, Officer Smith apprehended me. He ordered a breathalyzer test, to say the ABC's, and to walk a straight line. My breathalyzer registered a 1.4. I was .4 over Michigan's intoxication limit.

Until that moment, I had always supported law enforcement. I was definitely guilty of driving over the legal limit but not of the second charge: attempting to bribe the officer. That was an outright lie. I had been so nervous I removed my driver's license and a hundred dollar bill fell out at the same time. That hundred wasn't a bribe; it was the money I had saved for our last day of golf and gas for the trip home.

I had to stay in jail for six hours. Apparently, it takes one hour per drink to get alcohol completely out of the system. I figured it was a good thing that I had been driving. My friends would have had to spend weeks in jail to get rid of all the alcohol they had consumed that night. The four-and-one-half-hour ride home alone was anything but cheerful.

I eventually received a letter indicating a court date in Gaylord. When the date was set, I put on a new three-hundred-dollar suit and prepared to meet the honorable Judge Paula Manson. The appearance followed normal protocol. When I had my chance to speak, I said, "I thought I was okay, ma'am, and wanted to make sure everyone got home safely." I was pretty sure I had talked myself out of the situation, so I expected a slap on the wrist and a release.

Judge Manson said, "Sir, if you felt okay, perhaps you have a drinking problem." What a waste of a three-hundred-dollar suit. I could have worn a t-shirt. The aftershock included higher insurance rates, a hefty fine, and probation. Gaylord was not in Marquette County, so I didn't have to worry that anyone would read about the incident in the local newspaper.

My lifestyle didn't change. Even in my drunken stupor, I had signals about some bedrock problems with Angie: she kept her own maiden name after we were married, and we always had to schedule expensive vacations. Of course, I didn't pay attention to those signals. By 1998, my business fell 62 percent when new insurance regulations hindered profit, prompting many insurance companies to leave Michigan. We had to curb our extravagant lifestyle, and Angie was told we wouldn't be taking any more vacations until business picked up. Shortly thereafter, Angie left the marriage. I stayed in a half-vacant house with our dog, Misty.

If that wasn't enough to drive me to despair, the wood structure of the house basement started collapsing due to incompetent carpentry—something about forgetting to nail all the boards. I confronted the builder to return my $8,000 land contract down payment and to take the house back. I hired an attorney and stopped making house payments. The builder was forced to take the house back, I saved $8,200 dollars in payments, and the judge awarded me $3,000. I was once again divorced and without a home. My life was gambling, drinking, and playing hockey. My secretary, Darlene, kept our business going while I drove around The Upper Peninsula making service calls as fast as possible so I could get to the nightlife. Did I even know where my daughters were?

My doctor put me on an antidepressant. The first pill was a little too strong. I was so relaxed I think I asked Misty to drive one night. The doctor modified my medication, and I was off again.

One night, I decided to drive twenty-seven miles to Marquette to party. After singing karaoke in Flannigan's Bar and not drinking much, I decided it was time to return home. At the crossroads, a four-corner stop, I saw a Michigan state police car on my left. Feeling very confident, I pulled out first and continued to drive the last fourteen miles home. Misty was with me, and approximately six miles down the road, Misty decided that she wanted to sit on my lap. When she moved, my car veered a little, and the flashing red lights went on. Here we go again.

I had to pass all of the same tests as the previous time in Gaylord. I registered another 1.4 and was off to the "sin bin" again. I refused to go unless the officer drove Misty to a friend's house. Fortunately, he did. I was booked and spent another night in jail—this time with a group of friends from the local casino. Guilty as charged. Jail time number three. When will I grow up? My answer was, "Who cares?" My daughters were not communicating with me. My only concern was to keep this a secret from Mom.

This time, the judge put the hammer down. The fines were large, my driving was now restricted, and I faced twelve weeks of classes on alcoholism. My insurance went up yet again, and I could only drive between 6:00 a.m. and 12:00 p.m. That allowed me time to work. What now?

My life was under heavy scrutiny of an irresponsible behavior. I need to slow down and develop a purpose in life. I had a close friend, Marcia Lawton, who lived nearby and was raising two very active boys as a single mom. The boys were Anthony and Jonathan.

I joined Marcia's life. She was the widow of my good friend Mark, and I was the godfather to the youngest boy, Anthony. Because the older boy's godparents were in Texas, I assumed that role also. These boys filled a large void, as I missed my daughters so much.

One night, in January of 1999, Anthony, Jonathan, and I attended a college hockey game in Marquette. It was that night that a friend, Danielle Smith, told me about Angela. Not Angie; Angela. How ironic? Having two women with the same name was real convenient. I have been told I talk in my sleep.

ROCK CLIMBING ONCE AGAIN

Big Shag Lake in Gwinn, Michigan, was advertising homes for sale in my price range. If I was more alert, my price range would have been zero. I found a great house about 150 feet from the lake. The backyard was fenced in, and the back door had a little opening, a doggy door for Misty. The Back Door Lodge was near, a "watering hole" for me. Misty was allowed in, and she immediately handled floor maintenance She loved popcorn. The surroundings were perfect: I could drink, take Misty with me, and live a secluded life in the woods. I bought the house.

Reluctantly, I let Angela in my life. She was a divorced woman who had been married twenty-five years to a Pentecostal pastor. For four years, Angela surprised me. She was like a soul mate if a sixty-two-year-old knows what that is. She was perfect for me.

God has always been number one in my life. When I was fifteen, I took to heart the message to be positive person. In September of 2001, I experienced another tremendous revelation, the kind of revelation nondenominational churches refer to as being "born again." Angela and I were sitting in church at 11:07 a.m. It was September 21, 2001, when, during prayer with my eyes closed, I saw a large door open. I felt a tremendous power sweeping through my body. The doors changed my entire attitude. Everything from swear words to the taste of alcohol no longer felt good to me. It was like I had no control over these changes. I did feel reborn and vowed to make a 100 percent commitment to following the Word. I would no longer live with a six-pack in one Hand and a Bible in the other. I would moderate my life and continue to reach out to "lift every room."

There was tremendous peace. The pressure and sadness were not as dominating. Where would I go with my newfound message? Having so much experience as a church leader and watching so many lay approaches to worship God, I knew I would follow only Jesus. Watching very intently, I could see churches competing with each other to have the largest buildings and the most worshipers. I thought about God, religion, and my past. Religious and church leaders in the U.S. operated competitively; they were in business. While organized religion serves a purpose, I follow the Father, Son, and Holy Spirit without a middleman. The middleman is very important as a messenger of the Bible's history. I take the message to individual prayer to review with who? Jesus. Following people on earth is setting yourself up for failure and disappointment. Humans sin. I now believed that when my number was called, God would say, "What were you doing down there?" as Mr. Young writes, I believe. It was what I want to reflect. I believe God wants me to relax; enjoy; smell the roses; and most importantly, have a good heart.

At the time Angela came into my life, I was spiritually ready for a change from the Lutheran church. Angela was a Pentecostal Christian. I had no idea what that really meant. She took me to several churches. At one church, people were talking during the sermon, dancing, clapping, and using tongue language. *What a bunch of wackos*, I thought. The church service looked and sounded like a super bowl party full of drunken Green Bay Packer fans. That was not for me.

We finally settled on a non-denominational church with Pastor Mike Lawson, who, along with his wife, Suzette, would become good friends. When Mike and Suzette moved to Appelton, Wisconsin, in 2002, Angela and I followed to have Mike marry us.

Angela was exactly what I was looking for. She had evolved from the extremist behavior of a Pentecostal pastor's wife to a moderate Christian. She developed a sense of humor. She and I lived and loved a great life for four years. We had plenty of money. We enjoyed boating on the lake and celebrating holidays with her sons and their families. We purchased a large home on Big Shag Lake.

Before I married Angela, an auto salesman and friend of mine told me I was getting a wonderful woman if I could get past her sons. Again, I did not listen. I could get along with anyone.

Angela's behavior changed in the fifth year. Whatever her oldest son, Mitch, wanted, she agreed to. She almost had to. If Mitch didn't get his way, he took it. Compromise was out of the question. Angela's younger son, Dillon, worked in the business world and was the closest thing to moderate in the family. His wife, Aston, shared the same approach to life. He was extremely enjoyable to be around.

It was so obvious, being from a different upbringing, to see how all of us were raised differently. I only know one way: don't lie, cheat, or steal. That is my father to the extreme. I enjoyed watching Angela hide certain behaviors to maintain a religious moat. "Put the bottle of wine in the garage. My boys are coming over. Melvin you do not witness properly," I was instructed. I do miss most of their family. It was quite humorous for me to see so many family problems were about church. As Young states in his writings, God must be amused. In our own family, all the way back to my grandparents, the family is split over who attends what church. The church tells families how to raise children, how much to pay, what movies to watch, what schools to attend. My God loves and respects all.

We were married in 2002, and up to January of 2004, we were living on the lake in Michigan. In the winter, I played hockey in the NHL. The league has tremendous respect until people find out it is the Negaunee Hockey League named after a small town nine miles west of Marquette. Playing hockey wasn't easy. I had to drive thirty-five miles to get to the hockey arena and to dress for the game. The rink wasn't heated, some nights, the wind chill was −20 degrees. In addition, I had weak Legs that would require total knee replacements scheduled for 2010. I had to wrap them with gauze and tape before every game. Fully regaled in my hockey gear, I stood 6 feet 4 inches and weighed 240 pounds. Every time I stepped onto that ice, I felt a tremendous rush of adrenaline.

On January 25, 2004, while playing left wing in a game, I was checked into the boards by Donny McDougall, a man larger than me. My left leg snapped. It was my stronger leg. In 1984 my right knee had been operated on. I couldn't get up. I knew my hockey days were over.

The next morning, I scheduled an appointment with Dr. Pearson, an Orthopedic Surgeon. Six weeks later, I was able to see him. He first suggested that I try three injections of fluid in my legs. Every six weeks, I dutifully returned for some more lubrication. That helped for awhile, but surgery was inevitable. On my third and last visit, I told Dr. Pearson to operate on and replace both knees at the same time. He didn't advocate two replacements in one day because the pain would be unbearable and the rehabilitation long and difficult. I was a salesman, and I convinced him to replace both on October 4, 2004.

All necessary arrangements were made. My secretary could run the business, and a friend, Dennis Markula, would drive me to the rehab. Dr. Pearson enjoyed a fine reputation. I was ready.

The routine surgery wasn't routine. My left knee was so badly damaged that I was in surgery longer than anyone has anticipated. Once the longer-than-expected operation was completed, I woke up hooked up to a leg mobility machine. My legs were moving just as they would if I were riding a stationary bike. Angela visited me every day, and on day three, she read my charts. A nurse herself, Angela recognized Renal Failure. My liver and kidneys were shutting down, and my left lung collapsed. I was dying.

Angela used her knowledge and connections to contact Dr. Mark Cowan, a Cardiologist who was not In the hospital. She asked him to come as soon as possible. On his way to the hospital, Cowan called intensive care to obtain all of the equipment he needed to handle my emergency. He didn't expect me to live. I was in a coma, my heart was engulfed, crushed by seventy pounds of pressure. He gave me less than an hour to live and had some call my mother. Mom called Pastor Paul Marian. Dr. Cowan didn't believe he could save me but wanted to try one long shot: using the heart to restart the liver and kidneys.

I would experience my third revelation. It was moist in my coma—not warm or cold, just damp. I looked to my left and saw nothing. Then I got scared. I said, "Lord, where are the lights and the music of heaven?"

"You are not coming," He said. I was going to live. Dr. Cowan and Angela had saved my life. God didn't want me yet.

Angela didn't either. By May of 2006, Angela had changed. Mitch took command for her life, making insinuations to Angela that she should attend all family functions and that she should be more available. When Mitch and his family came over, he had very little respect for our home. It was Mitch's show. His mom went along with everything. I refused to get involve. Angela and I fought more and more. People close to me could not figure out if Angela was jealous because my disability kept me from working. I still contributed 40 percent of our income.

In 2005. I was in rehab and friends were assisting me. Angela and I had previously vacationed in Florida and decided we wanted to move there. I would stay in Michigan to finish therapy and to sell our lake home. Angela would work in a Florida Hospital and supervise the building of our new home. She would live in an apartment until the house was completed. I would fly down to see her as often as possible. I moved in the spring of 2006. The Michigan house did not sell before I left Michigan.

We fought a lot about money. The house in Michigan didn't sell, my Social Security Disability petition was denied, and, according to Angela, we were not saving or giving enough to the church. We decided to get counseling advice, both financial and personal. The financial counselors said we had a good ten-year plan, that all the problems would resolve themselves. Angela didn't want to wait. She wasn't around her family enough, we didn't have enough money, and she couldn't handle the stress.

FLORIDA'S SAND STARTS SHIFTING

My mother came to visit us in Florida each winter. My mother is a great person. When she feels good, she loves to cook and clean. She never offers us advice unless we solicit it. The only time Mom ever said anything was during our drive to Tampa airport. She said my marriage was deteriorating. She didn't want me to have to live in such a confrontational environment and would support anything I chose. I never realized that Angela and her son had already planned her escape route.

Angela traveled to Montana every year to see her family. This time, she stayed a little longer than expected. When she came home, I asked her how her trip was. She said, "Good. I am moving back." Her son, Mitch, had a duplex for her to live in, and she had already interviewed at a local hospital for a nurse's position. She was going back there—alone.

Angela's announcement was devastating. I wondered how we could lose a marriage in which God was so prevalent. After the shock of her plans settled down, we drew up a mutually agreed upon settlement. From February to May, Angela went to work, packed, and prepared for her move. Her sons would fly to Florida to drive a U-Haul back to Montana. I felt like a bobble head doll as I watched the preparation. Since the house in Florida was only in Angela's name, I would stay in it and refinance—if and when my disability claim was granted. She would leave Florida in April and would fly back for the three-minute divorce. I didn't attend the one-day divorce procedure. I received a letter from Angela, informing me that the divorce was final. She also told me that she was giving the house back to the bank since it made no sense for her to invest money in something she would never use.

    I shared the letter with Angela's loan officer, Jim Edgars. He asked me to stay in the house to keep it looking nice for sale. All I had to do was pay the utilities until he notified me to vacate. He wouldn't be able to help me, as I would have to make up the missed payments and make the taxes current. He advised me to move.

BEDROCK

God works in mysterious ways. I often wonder why the house in Michigan never sold while we were married, why my disability claim was taking so long, and why I was once again divorced and alone. The Bible instructs that I not be "anxious over anything." This Bible instruction is out of Philippians, verse 4. Sometimes, following that dictum wasn't easy. But another Bible instruction—everything comes to those who wait—was part of my faith, which never faltered. As soon as Angela left, everything fell into place. The bank took the Michigan house back and never foreclosed on me. I worked with them to sell the house. I was awarded social security disability. A friend found a place for me to live while I waited for my first disability check. My name would be cleared. I once again found solace and salvation in my Savior. He was watching over me—one set of footprints in the sand.

Throughout my life, I spent long hours trying to figure out what God was thinking when He made me. Sometimes, I wondered if he was concentrating. Confidence in everyday life was never a problem. I find it very difficult to understand why communication skills overshadow actual abilities. Many times, Fast Freddie would tell people I was the best Coach at our high school. In my heart, I knew that our basketball coach was much more knowledgeable than me. The difference was the presentation of the teachings. This was very stressful because my good, old conscience didn't feel it was right to excel above others because I could talk.

The biggest disappointment in life is what I call surface discernment. This also relates to my description of being a Christian. People who lack foundations are not truthful with the mirror and will only allow people and beliefs in their life that do not challenge their comfort zone. Along with this shifting comes joining and following structured programs that mirror behavior. In worship, I call this menu Christianity. To further define this would be to pray to God to bless lives. This is fine and falls into early Christianity. My question is, what do we do after the prayer? Be patient is an acceptable answer and one very prevalent in daily life. In the last two years, I have taken prayer to a different level.

As stated earlier in the reading and summarized now, I take a soft interpretation of the Book of Samuel. In layman's language I mean to pray for Jesus to take your prayers to the Father for guidance. Before I pray for something, I feel a responsibility to prepare the prayer. An example of this is to ask for guidance on the petitions you develop in life. It is not necessary to be sad if your prayers are not what you hoped for. Have faith. God will never hurt you. Have trust. Write on paper what your concerns are. Look at them everyday. Watch how each day's perception changes in pressure. This could be *the message* and you are being taught patience.

I live my life in moderation. I read funny jokes and not all are considered healthy. I like to have a glass or two of wine. Nothing too extreme. Once in awhile is great. I can't control others' behavior, and steps taken to hurt me are always reduced in pain by my relationship with Jesus. Why people harbor hard feelings is always going to be a mystery of me.

Surface Discernment is commonplace in most relationships. This term is better known as first impression. In my life, I have always said that 80 percent of people who meet me for the first time do not like me. In most cases, I become known and am found out to be a Teddy Bear. Remember, in my first revelation, I was asked to lift the room. This worked great in the world away from church. In fact, I am blessed with many friends. Once I retired, I found out that I come across like a control freak.

In a recent conversation, I approached someone I truly love and used my old technique. In business or coaching, a leader has to make quick, correct decisions. Making incorrect decisions will lead to you not leading or coaching. My technique was to bust them down first and then build them up. I brought that approach to my friend, who was not used to coaches and worldly leaders. I was disappointed that I didn't have as close a relationship with the man, a man of the cloth. I said, "I have been mad at you for many years, and now I am so happy with you. We could have had a great relationship for years if you would have been available." That approach went over like a pregnant Pole Vaulter. It was meant to be a compliment; but as I read it now, with my new personal awareness, it is pretty weak.

Being bullheaded is right on the top of my surface discernment. Go deeper in my life. You will find that I have a strong personality trait where I will not agree if I don't understand. Even though I graduated nineteenth in my high school class, I still have difficulty understanding certain behaviors. Reach deeper into what I Say, and you find that we only had twenty students in our class. Many only hear *nineteenth*.

The gifts God gives all of us vary in texture. I find that most people never solidify to the point where they can maximize all of their talents and desires. Living in America, a country built by entrepreneurs, gives all of us opportunities to shoot for the stars. What stops us is the dysfunction in childhood development that breeds insecurity about the future.

Being a parent, I can tell you that the choices each of us make for our families are based on what we have been taught. These choices come from the heart. Many children don't understand this until they become parents or until a tragedy occurs. I reconciled with my father on his seventieth birthday. The reunion was shocking. He told me that he wished he was more like me when he finally found the courage to sing in the church choir at age seventy. Then he cried. I spent most of my life feeling I wasn't living to my dad's standards.

Ego, conceit, and confidence are closely related emotions with very different connotations. When we have a solid foundation in life, there are no floods or winds that can move us. I am a very confident person. Actually, it is very easy to be confident. My ingredients are a strong relationship with Jesus, a great prayer format, and my father's teaching to *never* lie, cheat, or steal. At the surface, my confidence looks like stubbornness. Looking deeper, if I do not agree with what I am being told or I don't understand, I will not agree. In all reality, I wish more people could convince me with issues. I would prefer peace. I will always demand accuracy.

There have been people in my life who choose not to accept me. I have no problem with their positions. Over the years, I have been called a manipulator, pipe dreamer, a person who buys friends, and an overall control freak. Those accusations are true only in the perception of the believer. Looking deeper, you will find that my heart is not in those behaviors. I will control when it affects me or when I do not believe what is told to me. I have to be convinced before I agree. Take your pick: bull-headed, or conscientious. My feeling is bull-headed if I intimidate you, or conscientious if you are solid rock.

Choosing good means that all of the past should provide lessons for the future. If I could choose again, I would never have used alcohol as much as I did. Perhaps that outlet was the result of my "highly anxious" psyche and borderline depression. Each day, I have to work on being positive. The depression is still there, but now I embrace it. I live by believing that nothing has power but the power I give it. I fight daily to rob depression of controlling my life.

The three women in my life are wonderful people. It is never one person's fault for loss of marriage. Julie is beautiful, intelligent, and filled full of abilities that were not developed when we met. After twenty years together, I feel that she was unable to grow. My personality was so dominant and we were so short of being ready to get married that I overshadowed her. Our upbringings were similar: very conservative, driven by doctrine passed down through the Lutheran way.

Angie was 5 feet 2 inches, blonde, well proportioned, and very beautiful. When we met, she was a talented office manager with a high school education, completing duties that college graduates would struggle with. As a team, we worked on her self-confidence to the point where she eventually became the finance manager for a new four-star hotel in Marquette. The budget for the renovated hotel was put together so poorly before Angie was hired that when the local bank wanted a review, Angie represented the business. We used to laugh at home that it was a good thing that she finished high school. Only in America. What a country. I really enjoyed our eight years together.

Angela was forced on me by our mutual friend. That was a blessing. We had a rough first year, four great years, and then the previously described fallout related to family and faith. I learned a lot from Angela and miss many members of her family.

My relationship with Amy and Cory is distant. The church they attend is similar to the non denominational church Angela attends. These churches seem to have a menu driven by doctrine and influenced by laypeople trained as pastors or in leadership roles. I don't have a problem with teaching the Word. I get leery when personal discernment falls short. Just because the person you are with says something that does not sit well with you should intrigue more research to see if the idiot is truly an idiot. Look deeper.

I struggle with churches that try to control my life. I am looking for Biblical direction and good healthy worship music. When mention is made of other churches' worship procedure, when churches encourage full disclosure of your personal life to receive forgiveness, to raise your children the same as all, and to constantly stay in the church groups is when I ask "Where do you allow for reaching out to unbelievers?" Your pastor was trained for his position. A teacher is trained for their positions. My solution is to learn and discern. Then take it Prayer.

Where do parents fit in? I can't speak for the mother of Amy and Cory. I feel like our daughters are ashamed of me. The three divorces do not fit the cosmetic image necessary to rise in their circle. If there is pain from the original divorce, I would be willing to counsel to all levels to reach my most important desire in my life, that of being father and grandfather. Grandparents are extremely special. Cory and Amy are blessed to have a healthy, eighty-four-year-old grandmother. Each day their grandmother asks about the

family, distant for over two years. I don't know what to say. What bothers me most is what god or church would support that behavior.

My previous paragraph reflects on many families who have children in this generation. It is a nonpersonal generation tied together with computers, cell phones, etc. Do we have a right to want to be in our children's lives? At the age of thirty-eight I'm not sure I paid much attention to my parents. In hindsight, I wish I would have. Being a son of sixty-two and having a Mother of eighty-four is totally different. I speak to Mom daily about me, her granddaughters and families, and the Detroit Tigers.

When you have a life as I have described, there are many directions to take. Some don't believe I should be so open; others choose depression, negativity, harbor hard feelings, and on and on. I can only tell you that my Divine Interventions are imbedded in me. I am not asking all to be Christians because I truly believe God made all of us. Surface discernment will try to label me. That will not work because Jesus died for my sins, so I have chosen openness to reach out to show people that no past behaviors stay when you reach out for forgiveness and there are no embarrassments in life when you follow the Word. If you would like advice, start with liking what you see in the mirror. The mirror does not lie. Next, follow my paternal father—never lie, cheat, or steal. Start slow, and be consistent.

Love is something that I have come to understand only recently. Believing in the Father, Son, and Holy Spirit solidifies my soul. Living a life where I understand anxiety (Philippians) and not chasing my concerns (Samuel) works for me.

The phone is ringing. Maybe it's one of my daughters.

Melvin John Ruohonen commonly referred to as Mel was born and raised in the Upper Peninsula of Michigan. Graduating from Kindergarten in Hancock, Michigan, Mel, and family (Mom and Dad). Moved to a Mining Community of White Pine, Michigan where graduation took place in 1965.

At age sixty-three, Mel began reflecting on his life and was encouraged to write a book. Now, seventy-three years old, a second review of the book's contents, Mel realized the message is best fitted to 2021. From Shifting Sand to Solid Rock relates to Youth from the 60's, most with foundations, are better reflected in 2021. The way my age group dealt with problems (opportunities) was to fall back on our Foundations. What do today's youth use as a benchmark to reach Solid Rock?

I strongly believe today is addressed for all ages in the words. To further enjoy reading put your life in the life of the Author, be Empathetic to the Deep, honest reflection of both age groups.

To fully understand Melvin John, please refer to THE AUTHOR. THE BUTTERFLY. THE BOOK. The entire chapter, plus POEM is a reflection of a friend of 30 years, Jeannie Milakovich, most accurately, my neighbor. The Poem is my inspiration every time I read the Script. Jeannie was an English Teacher in a local Junior College.

Viet Nam was in a "hot war" and I was Lotto Number 109, our countries Draft Program, due to join the Armed Forces in June '65. Walter Cronkite, CBS News Anchor announced that "there will be no further Draftees for Ontonagon County in Michigan as 13 young Men's lives were taken up to that point, "a large percentage from a small county. Being an only child, my parents wanted me to attend College. I attended Northern Michigan University with a Degree in Education and an extensive music background playing the Trumpet, I joined NMU's Marching and Concert Band. The Book will continue with ALL careers from 1970 – 2021.

During this time from 1965 to current, I encourage to play the Devil's Advocate, are you in the Book? Life has "Ups and Downs". Remember take your opportunities (problems) eliminate Emotion, and "Never leave the mirror in the morning until you see something you like".

www.ingramcontent.com/pod-product-compliance
Ingram Content Group UK Ltd.
Pitfield, Milton Keynes, MK11 3LW, UK
UKHW022217230426
12048UKWH00016BA/893